INSTRUMENTS
in
MUSIC

CLASSICAL MUSIC

Roger Thomas

Heinemann Library
Des Plaines, Illinois

Designed by Susan Clarke
Printed in Hong Kong

02 01 00 99 98
10 9 8 7 6 5 4 3 2 1

Library of Congress Cataloging-in-Publication Data

Thomas, Roger, 1956-
 Classical music / Roger Thomas.
  p. cm. — (Instruments in music)
 Includes bibliographical references and index.
 Summary: Introduces some of the instruments used in classical
music, including the violin, trumpet, and flute, as well as early
instruments.
 ISBN 1-57572-641-6 (lib. bdg.)
 1. Musical instruments—Juvenile literature. [1. Musical
instruments.] I. Title. II. Series.
ML460.T4 1998
784.16'8—dc21   97-49505
                                                                          CIP
                                                                    MN AC

Acknowledgements
The Publishers would like to thank the following for permission to reproduce photographs:
Bridgeman Art Library, p.6; Trevor Clifford, pp.20 top and middle, 22, 23, 25 (Hertfordshire County Music Service),
pp.8, 10 left (Hill & Company), pp.10 right, 12, 15 right (John Myatt Brass and Woodwind), pp.5, 7 bottom left and
bottom right, 9, 11, 13, 14, 19, 20 bottom, 21 (The Purcell School), p.26 Yamaha-Kemble Music (UK); Liz Eddison, p.7
bottom middle, p.7 top right and middle right, (Hobgoblin Music); Chris Honeywell, p.7 top left, p.24; Redferns, pp.26,
28, 29, (Henrietta Butler), p.18, (Odile Noel), p.4 (David Redfern); Trip, p.15 (B. Gibbs), p.17 (H. Rogers); Yamaha,
p.15 left (Rob Wyatt); Zefa, p.16.

Cover photograph: Redferns/Barbara Steinwehe

Our thanks to Betty Root for her comments in the preparation of this book.
Every effort has been made to contact copyright holders of any material reproduced in this book. Any omissions will
be rectified in subsequent printings if notice is given to the Publisher.

Any words appearing in bold, **like this,** are explained in the Glossary.

CONTENTS

INTRODUCTION

This book is about the instruments used in classical music. This music began about two hundred years ago. The instruments can all be played in a big group called an orchestra which is usually led by a conductor. The conductor leads the muscicians and helps them all play together. He usually marks the time of the music with a stick called a baton.

This orchestra includes every type of instrument in this book!

This group is playing chamber music.

Classical instruments are often played in smaller groups called ensembles or chamber groups. "Chamber" is an old word for room. It is called chamber music because it could be performed in an ordinary room without needing a big concert hall. Many instruments are also played with just a piano or sometimes by themselves.

INSTRUMENTS IN EARLY MUSIC

Concert music was played for about three hundred years before classical music began. This music is now called early music. It is still performed today.

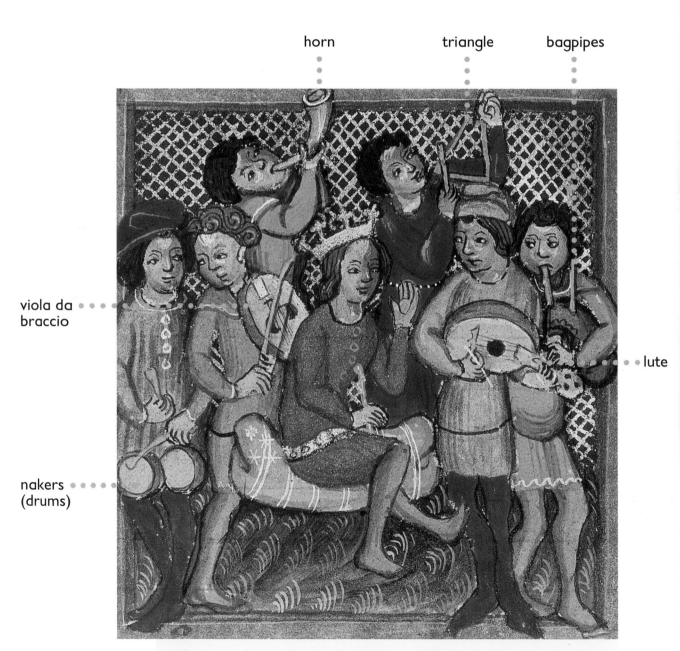

horn   triangle   bagpipes

viola da braccio

lute

nakers (drums)

These instruments were used in concert music.

Instrument makers changed the way the instruments were made as the years went by until they were like the instruments in this book. All the instruments shown below are based on the early instruments shown on the facing page.

viola

French horn

triangle

bagpipes

timpani

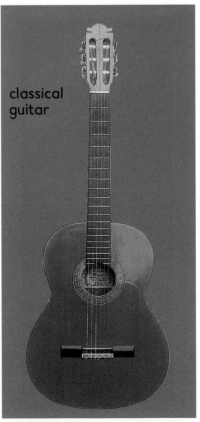
classical guitar

THE VIOLIN AND VIOLA

The violin and viola are stringed instruments made of wood. They each have four strings. The player strokes the strings with the **hair** on a **bow** which makes the strings sound. The strings can also be plucked with the fingers. The player changes the **notes** by holding the strings down on the **neck** of the instrument.

The violin and the viola

violin   viola

The violin has a clear, bright tone. The viola is more gentle.

The violin is the classical stringed instrument which plays the highest notes. The viola plays slightly lower notes. They are played by resting them on the player's shoulder. The player holds the instrument in place with his or her chin.

THE CELLO AND DOUBLE BASS

The cello and double bass are also stringed instruments made of wood. The cello has four strings. The double bass usually has four but can sometimes have five. The player strokes the strings with the **hair** on a **bow** to make the strings sound or plucks them with his or her fingers. The player changes the **notes** by holding the strings down on the **neck** of the instrument.

cello

double bass

A cello and a double bass

The cello and the double bass have a
smooth, mellow tone.

The cello has a low pitch but the double bass has the
lowest pitch of all the classical string instruments. The
cellist sits down to play. The cello has a **spike** which the
player rests on the floor. The double bass player either
stands up to play or sits on a high stool.

THE FLUTE AND PICCOLO

The flute and piccolo are woodwind instruments, although most modern flutes are made of metal. The player makes them sound by blowing air across a hole in a **mouthpiece** while pressing **keys** on the instrument. The keys cover and uncover holes along the instrument which let the air out in different places. This changes the **notes**.

A flute and a piccolo

flute

piccolo

A musician who plays a flute is called a flautist.

The piccolo plays higher notes than the flute. There are other flutes which play lower notes—the alto flute and the bass flute. Flautists often have to know how to play more than one kind of flute.

THE CLARINET, OBOE, AND BASSOON

The clarinet is a woodwind instrument, but some clarinets are made of plastic. The player blows into a **mouthpiece** which has a single **reed**. The reed makes the sound and the player changes the **notes** by covering holes and pressing **keys** on the instrument with his or her fingers. The clarinet has a sweet, lively **tone**.

There are several different sizes of clarinet.
The bigger clarinets play lower notes.

Oboe and bassoon players blow into two reeds which are
tied tightly together. The reeds make a sharp, clear sound.
The players change the notes by pressing keys which cover
and uncover holes on the instruments. The oboe plays
higher notes than the bassoon. A similar instrument,
called a cor anglais or English horn, plays notes which are
higher then the bassoon but lower than the oboe.

oboe

bassoon

The oboe and bassoon are both
double-reed woodwind instruments.

THE TRUMPET AND FRENCH HORN

The trumpet and French horn are both **brass** instruments. They are made of metal tubes. They make a sound when the player presses his or her lips tightly together and blows into the **mouthpiece** on the instrument.

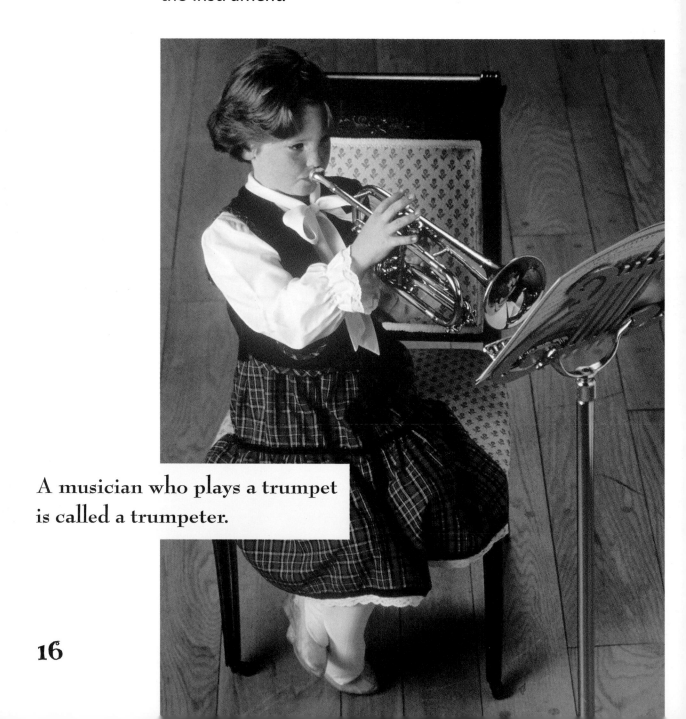

A musician who plays a trumpet is called a trumpeter.

A musician who plays a French horn is called a horn player.

The player changes the **notes** on these instruments with his or her lips and by pressing **valves** on the instrument. The valves let air into different lengths of tube. The trumpet has a sharp, clear **tone** and a high pitch. The French horn has a lower pitch and a smoother tone.

THE TUBA AND TROMBONE

The tuba is a **brass** instrument which plays low **notes**. It is made of a metal tube. It makes a sound when the player presses his or her lips together and blows into a **mouthpiece**. The player changes the notes with his or her lips and by pressing **valves** on the instrument. This lets air into different pieces of the tube.

This musician is playing a tuba.

18

This musician is
a trombonist.

The trombone is also a brass instrument. It plays notes
which are lower than the French horn but higher than the
tuba. Its sound is made in the same way as the other
brass instruments. To change the notes, the player moves
a piece of U-shaped tube called a slide. This makes the
notes higher or lower.

TUNED PERCUSSION

glockenspiel

Tuned percussion can be used to add different kinds of sounds to classical music. Because these instruments have **notes** like a piano, they can play tunes. They are played by tapping the bars on the instrument with hard or soft **beaters**.

xylophone

The glockenspiel, xylophone, and marimba are all tuned percussion instruments.

marimba

A person who plays percussion instruments is called a percussionist.

The glockenspiel has small metal bars. It has a clear, ringing **tone**. The xylophone has small wooden bars. It has a sharp, hard tone. The marimba has bigger wooden bars. It plays lower notes than the xylophone. It has long tubes which hang underneath the bars. These give the instrument a warm, full tone.

UNTUNED PERCUSSION

Untuned percussion instruments each have their own special sound but the player cannot play tunes on them. Lots of different untuned percussion instruments can be used in classical music. In some pieces of music the percussionist even has to play things which are not real instruments at all, such as scrap metal or car horns!

tam-tam

cymbals

bass drum

triangle

tenor drum

side drum

tambourine

woodblock

whip

flexatone

vibraslap

This percussionist has many different instruments to play.

A percussionist can make lots of sounds with untuned percussion instruments. The instruments include drums, a tambourine which makes a jingling sound, cymbals which make a crashing sound and a metal triangle which makes a high-pitched sound.

TIMPANI

Timpani are big metal drums shaped like bowls. They play very low **notes** and make a deep booming sound. They are usually played with soft **beaters**. Timpani are usually played in sets of two or three, but some music needs as many as sixteen! Timpani are sometimes called kettledrums.

A pair of timpani

A drummer who plays timpani is called a timpanist.

On modern timpani the timpanist can change the notes by pressing a pedal underneath the drum. This makes the **skin** of the timpani tighter. The tighter the skin, the higher the note. A pointer with the notes marked on it shows which note the drum will play. On old timpani the notes were changed by screws, which took a lot longer.

THE PIANO AND THE HARP

In classical music, the piano can be played by itself or with one or more other instruments or singers. It is often played at the front of an orchestra, or further back as a part of the orchestra. A piano makes a sound when the player presses the **keys**. This makes soft **hammers** hit strings inside the instrument.

This pianist is playing some music for **solo** piano.

This harpist is playing in an orchestra.

The harp is usually played as part of an orchestra but it can be played by itself or in smaller groups. The player plucks the strings with his or her fingers to play the **notes**. Some of the notes can be changed with pedals pressed by the player's feet. The pedals stretch some of the strings. The harp has a soft, gentle sound.

CLASSICAL SINGING

Singing is used in classical music in lots of ways. A singer can sing **solo** with a piano, small group or orchestra. Many singers together are called a choir or chorus. Some music is written for choir and **soloists**. Classical singers need strong, specially-trained voices.

A solo singer

This opera chorus has many singers.

An opera is al kind of play which is written for singers with an orchestra, instead of for actors. All the words are usually sung by soloists, with a chorus of many other voices.

GLOSSARY

beaters   sticks with rounded ends used for playing timpani and other percussion instruments

bow   a curved wooden stick with hair stretched along it for playing stringed instruments

brass   a type of hard metal used for making certain kinds of wind instruments

concert music   music written for performing in front of an audience

hair   used on bows for stringed instruments. The hair is covered with a sticky substance which makes the strings sound when it is rubbed across them. Bow hair can be taken from a horse's tail or from plastic

hammers   wooden sticks covered in soft felt which are found inside a piano. These hit strings inside the instrument to make them sound

keys   the black and white levers on a piano keyboard which the player presses with his or her fingers to make the notes, or the metal buttons on a woodwind instrument which move pads covering holes on the instrument

mouthpiece   the part of a wind instrument which the player blows into

neck   a long piece of wood on a stringed instrument which the strings are stretched along

notes   musical sounds

reed   a thin piece of cane in the mouthpiece which makes the sound on a clarinet, oboe, and bassoon

skin   the covering on timpani made from calfskin or plastic

solo   one musician playing or singing

soloist   a performer with an important part to play or sing alone in a piece of music

spike   a thin, pointed metal rod on the bottom of a cello which the player rests on the floor while playing

tone   whether a sound is soft and smooth or hard and bright

untuned   a kind of instrument which does not make clear notes

valves   buttons on a brass instrument which help to change the notes

MORE BOOKS TO READ

Delafosse, Claude. *Musical Instruments.* New York: Scholastic Inc. 1994.

Pillar, Marjorie. *Join the Band!* New York: Harper Collins Children's Books. 1994.

Susen, Phyllis B., ed. *Sound all Around.* Philadelphia: Philadelphia Orchestra Assn. 1992.

Staples, Danny & Mahoney, Carole. *Flutes, Reeds & Trumpets.* Fresno, CA: Millbrook Press. 1992.

INDEX